SOUL SEARCHING COLLECTION

ARTHUR L. BROWN

Table of Contents

INTRODUCTION

My passion for writing has always been somewhere trapped in my heart and mind. One day in late March 1995 I decided to write some poetry; however, my thoughts were centered around spiritual, historical, and cultural poetic messages. This approach would be the defining moment that launched a lifetime pursuing my dream of becoming an author with different genres combined not only in poetry but novels and autobiographies.

The following collection of poetic messages along with images relating stories of pass and present life events; allow me to present my Soul Searching Collection.

Chapter I

SOUL SEARCHING
THE CREATION

Creation

When God created the world
He carved it with his hands
He gave the animals life
From the dirt he made man

He placed them in a garden
He gave man control
He gave all freedom
But he gave man the soul

They lived their lives together
There was no hate or strife
But man was still lonely
Until God made him a wife

One day the devil came
Tempting with a lie
When they disobeyed God
They both had to die

They tried to hide their faces
They tried to run away
They covered their bodies in shame
We are still dying today

We are born in sin
From start to the end
It is very sad to say
We all came this way.

THE GOLDEN CITY

The Golden City

From heaven above the city came
It was built for all mankind
In this city God has fame
In it there's peace to find.

John saw the city coming down
Dressed like a bride so fine
The city was beautiful all around.
The greatest sight of all time.

In the city the people stood.
Praising God all day
When the book was open for the good
The sinners had nothing to say.

From the pit of hell the sinners cried
Following the world is how they died
They did not believe the city was real
They travel their own way

You don't want to know how they feel
If you want to live in the city one day.

SOUL SEARCHING
SALVATION

Salvation

From a time not forgotten, we all came.
God delivered us upon eagle's wings,
He eased our suffering; he cleared our way,
He gave us hope for a better day.

He sat upon a great mountain and looked down below,
He sat forth a direction for all of us to go.

He gave sight to the blind,
He made the lame walk,
He spoke the word and the dumb talked.

He reached out his hand to hold us close.
He sent Jesus the one he loved the most.

Jesus loves us dearly, but God loves best.
When your time is over go home and take your rest.

Merry Christmas

Happy Holidays

Christmas Day

On Christmas Day the people play
They eat and drink all day
They tell the story of unselfish glory
Born in a manger

He is no stranger
To all that love and pray

When Mary conceived
No one believed
That Jesus was coming soon
The day he was born in to life's storm
The angels played a tune.

The wise men came to see his fame
The animals bowed down to his crown
The heavenly host proclaims
Only once a year, you hear a cheer
From all that remain

Christmas Day! Oh, by the way
Is holy, sacred and blessed
When and if you see it again
Don't forget to pray my friend
God sent his best.

The Light

The Light

The Light came down from heaven
It conquered hate and strife
It built a great foundation
It gave eternal life

It set the captives free
Made way for you and me
It was bread for the hungry
It was sight for the blind
It was water for the thirsty
It shines on all mankind

If you cannot see it
When it passes your way
If you don't believe it
Wait until judgement day

The light will be shining
The way shall be clear
The light will be the judge
There is no need to fear

We cannot avoid it
Please don't even try
It has keys to salvation
It controls the reason why

Chapter II

SOULSEARCHING
KNOWLEDGE
Plus
UNDERSTANDING
Equals
SUCCESS
STAY IN
SCHOOL

Stay in School

The Army is not the only place
To be all you can be
Even though you travel a lot
The world you can see

If you stay in school
Read all that you can
Listen to your parents
Grow up to be a man

No one said life was easy
Sometimes not even fair
Everyone doesn't hate you
Some people really care

We all are pilgrims on the earth
Traveling the sea of time
God gave us rules
To keep all of us in line

The NBA is ok
The NFL too
They both are like the Marine Corps
They only take a few

Playing sports is good
It keeps the body fit
Don't forget to use your mind
Books are very cool

Computers now rule the day
You must stay in school.

SOUL SEARCHING

OUT OF CONTROL

Out of Control

The sun came up this morning
The rain stayed away
I was very happy to see another day
I picked up the newspaper
I looked through and through
There was no surprise - there was nothing new
The headlines labeled murder, on every page I read
Young and old people - representing the dead
Crime is all around us, and steadily on the rise
No one went to jail this is no surprise.

SOUL SEARCHING
THE STORM

The Storm

When the wind comes in rushing
Sweeping like a broom
The weather is changing fast
Nature is playing a tune
trees are busy dancing
Moving from side to side
The grass is lying down
animals go to hide
rain is coming soon
thunder leads the way
flowers are in full bloom
Another stately day
lightning shows its face
clouds are dark and gray
raindrops are keeping pace
The storm is on its way
first sign of darkness
The loud majestic sound
At the end there's rainbow
Such beauty seldom found

SOUL SEARCHING
THE
WRONG
TURN

The Wrong Turn

I woke up this morning in jail
There was no one to pay my bail
I worked in the streets day and night
I did not run from any fight

I hustled my people
I would back a friend
The money was good
There was no end

I loved every cutie pie that I saw
I had no regard for the law
In my mind I was king
I woke up this morning from a bad dream

The streets were cold
The money was gone
There is no gold
I'm in jail all – alone

SOUL SEARCHING

CHILDREN

Children

When I was a child
I spoke as a child
I stayed out of grown-ups face

When I broke the rule
My father was cool
He would put me back in my place

But now today! Oh! By the way.
Children don't care what they say
They do what they want
The family has gone astray
Don't blame the teacher
Forget about the preacher
The law rules today

You must bend the tree when it is young
You deal with problems when they come

It's up to you to see them through
They'll break your heart from the start
As we go on we must be strong
Parents must be bold
They must take control

SOUL SEARCHING
LOVE YOU MOM

Mother

She brought you to this world
Every boy and every girl
She makes the sacrifice
All of her life

She works every day
No matter come what may
She deals with the blame
She takes on the shame

She bares a lot of pain
Sometimes the way is hard
She's searching for her God
She knows he'll give her strength
Her days may be of length
Her family is her life
She makes the sacrifice

SOUL SEARCHING
My
Hero
LOVE YOU DAD

Father

He brings the bread home
He gives up his time
He keeps the kids in line
He works around the home

He works night and day
He pays the bills
He leads the way
He follows God
From the start
He must stay strong
Some days are long

Chapter III

HAPPY MARTIN LUTHER KING DAY

I Wonder What Martin Would Say

Martin Luther King had a dream,
for all mankind to be free.
He gave his life, The Greatest Sacrifice,
he died for you and me.

He wanted to right a wrong for freedom song,
for the entire world to see.
He went to jail; he did not fail to change history.

But now that he's gone we still sing the song, that
"We Shall Overcome."
But now today, Oh! by the way nothing has changed it's
still the same in freedoms name, life is a game that
people play.

Our children are dying,
Mothers are crying.

There is no hope except for hope,
that's in our neighborhoods.

The old folks are afraid to go outside,
Our people don't have any pride.
In the homes the men are gone
Our churches are dying too.

Oh! by the way I wonder what Martin would say,
Someone cried would he have died if he knew things
would end up this way.

HAPPY MARTIN LUTHER KING DAY

Love Passed Us By

For hundreds of years we were divided
Let's get together someone decided

For a moment, we came together
To fight for the same cause

We struggled and died to change the laws

Now we are back in bonds again
It is hard to find a brother
It is hard to find a friend

Our people are scattered
But does it really matter
We can't stay together
I wonder why

Someone said love passed us by

CELEBRATE BLACK HISTORY
HISTORY
Great Grand
Grand
Dad & Mom
Me
Mine
FAMILY
ROOTS
- SOUL SEARCHING

Family Roots

I found a tree by the riverside
It had many branches growing wide
It stood very tall in the dirt
It was deep rooted beneath the earth

I wish I could be like that tree
It hasn't been long since I've been free
Very little of my past is known
It has been this way since I was grown

I teach my children all that I can
I live my life like a man
Somewhere lost back in time
You'll find the reason and the rhyme

Yesterday long ago
You don't have to wonder no more
They scattered the babies everywhere
Who were the parents?
No one care

Someday I'll find my own bloodline
One day before the end of time
I will be able to look back
To see the mark of my own track

CELEBRATE BLACK CULTURE
CULTURE
WAKE
UP
- SOUL SEARCHING

Wake Up

It is time to see a brand new day
Open your eyes and look around
The sun no longer has its way
The sky is falling down

The time has come to except your end
In this life you can't pretend
We have failed our God
Pray to him a new start

Our children are dying everyday
Mothers are crying in every way
I never thought the day would come
When old folks out live the young

The young men are traveling their own way
The young ladies have a lot to say
Living false hopes and shattered dreams
Living in the dark-so it seems

Listen to the cry of a lonely child
Look at the mother when she style
Traveling in circles
Going nowhere
Who's looking— do you care

You left the women looking for gold
You left your babies in the cold
Your only way out is death or jail
You never knew the God you failed
Wake up and face the final fate
You have a chance
It's not too late

CELEBRATE BLACK CULTURE
THE OAK TREE
- SOUL SEARCHING -

The Oak Tree

In the middle of the road the Oak Tree stand
The shadow of the great oak covers the land
The branches are large, strong, and wide

It splits the road into two sides
Its roots are deep beneath the earth
Creating tunnels in the dirt.

On the branches rope strands clings
Roots so long they reach the stream
Leaves come and then they go
Covering the ground down below.

Stories are told of hanging men
In a time of hate and sin
In a time to be no more
Count the strands, then add the score.

Many have cried at the base of the tree
Many have died longing to be free.

Human fruit hanging from the vine
In this story no peace to find
The oak tree was innocent at a time so mean
It lead the way for freedom to ring.

CELEBRATE BLACK HISTORY

SOUL SEARCHING

Cotton Fields

One day we crossed the sea in shame
Tied to each other -- who's to blame
Made to work all day for free
Go to sleep tired as can be

Daylight comes very soon
Sun gets hot just before noon
Cotton rows very long
Might as well sing a song

Sing all day - don't worry about pay
The lord is watching everything
Why do people act so mean?
Cotton getting very tall
I'll be working in the gin this fall

A snake is lying in the middle of the row
Big mama killed him with a hoe
The people are praying for a breeze
Nothing but cotton - there are no trees
The dirt under my feet is very hot
I'm looking for a shady spot
The boss is looking at the ground
The children are chopping the cotton down
He yells with a loud voice to the crowd
Send the kids to the bus
I see no one is feeling proud
Then he began to cuss

Everyone heard what he said
No one out here is afraid
Big mama said boy - let's go
Down we went - down the cotton row

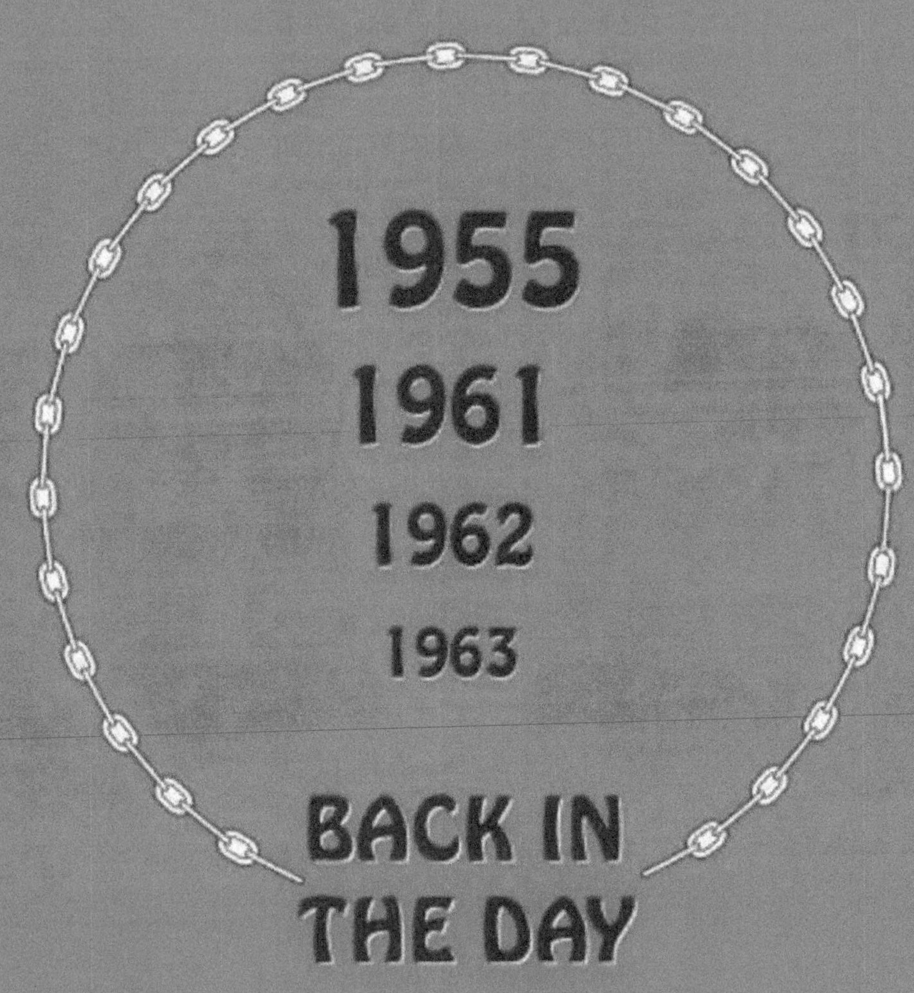
CELEBRATE BLACK CULTURE
1955
1961
1962
1963
BACK IN
THE DAY
- SOUL SEARCHING -

Back in the Day

Back in the day—people say
The time was good
In the neighborhood
We had control
Respected the old
The children could run and play

Remember the times—when things were fine
The old folks had something to say
Things have changed
People are strange Can you show me the way?

I woke up lost
I paid the cost
I could be wrong
I still sing the song
That we shall overcome We have to try Sometimes we cry
The race, we still must run

Chapter IV

The Prophecy

In a time far away, when kings ruled the day.
They travel near and far, guided by a star.
They looked for a child, born to rule a while.
The baby was born at night, under a sky so bright.

In a pile of hay, the Savior of the world lay.
There was no place at the Inn, not even a servant's den.
The shepherds saw the light, they talked to the angels that night.

The animals gather around, to see the Holy Crown.

The way for him was paved, he came to cheat the grave.
He came to lead the way; he'll judge the world one-day.

He came to save the lost; he paid the highest cost.
He taught us to pray, he said love is the way.

A Friend

When you need someone to listen
When you need someone to share
When you face trials and tribulations
You want someone to be there

When the storms of life are raging
When you reach your very end
Man will forsake you
Let Jesus be your friend

He will listen to your problems
He will answer all your prayers
He will love you forever
Because he really cares

He will give you comfort
He will ease all your fears
He will keep his arms around you
He will wipe away your tears

He will forgive all of your sins
Let him be your friend
When others turn away
He'll be there every day.

Birds

Birds talk all day
In a very special way
We try to understand
We listen very close
The crow talks the most

The eagle seldom seen
The buzzard spreads his wings

The hawk is looking down
There is prey to be found

The turkey walks the land
The jaybird is the man

The others fly the play
The sparrow leads the way

The redbird looks the best
They all have a nest.

Blessings

Before you ask your father for anything
What on the table did you bring?
Did you forget you had to pay?
What have you done for God today?

The servants obey his masters will
He's faithful, tried, and true
All of his time he freely gives
Now! What are you planning to do?

Are you looking for something?
Do you plan to give?
I know that you don't have nothing
You don't have a place to live

Blessings all come from God
You have to earn them from the start
If you treat your neighbors like a friend
God will bless you until the end

Choices

The mind is a home where good and evil may live
The heart is a place for all love to give
Your emotions controls your actions
The mind governs them all
You can survive any pressure
No matter how great or small

You set your mind on Jesus
Say no to the flesh
Keep your thoughts on salvation
Then take the final test
Live your life in goodness
Forget about the rest.

Courage

If you believe in God
If you trust in his son
Fear has no place
The battle has been won

Your enemies are your footstool
Those that hate you can see
The spirit of the Lord makes you free

You can climb any mountain
You can hold your head up high
You can demand respect
Until the day you die.

Don't Cry For Me

When time is over for me
There is a place I long-to be

My home is waiting in the sky
I have a home
It's way up high

Above the clouds
You cannot see
This place is for you
It is waiting for me

Where believers live
Forever to be free
Where dreams come true
The prophet knew

The place prepared long ago
Where hate and sin
Will be no more

Where angles sing
When freedom ring
Where the master live
With love to give
We all can claim
In Jesus name

Don't Forget to Pray

Time ran out this morning
The sun refuses to shine
The day will not be dawning
There is no more time

The end will soon be here
There will be no more tomorrow
The skies will not be clear
Oh! By the way
Did you forget to pray

There will be no more heat
Forget about the cold
Concentrate on Jesus
The Savior of your soul

Set your mind on him
There is a price to pay
We all can be saved
But don't forget to pray

Don't Weep for Me

I learned to follow Jesus
He is showing me the way
God sent him to free us
I'll see him judgement day

He knows my heart already
He cares about my pain
He heard me say this morning
I want to live again

He said speak the truth
Love God with all your heart
My works are not enough
I have tried to live my part

Born in a world of sin
Some days are really hard
One day it will end
I am going home to live with God.

Fear

Fear is a tool the devil uses
It causes hurt and pain

Designed to keep you confused
There is nothing to be gained

It won't take long before hate steps in
Hate can upset your very soul
It destroys the young
It destroys the old

Fear can lead to death
There is nothing to fear
Except fear itself

Follow the World

When man forgets the knowledge of God
He condemn himself from the start

When he decides to walk his own way
The final test on judgement day

Wayfarer travelers borrowing time
On the earth no peace to find

When time shall be no more
The game is over final score
To all players of Life final sacrifice

Chapter V

Follow Your Dream

Old men have visions
Young men dream dreams
Society say work as a team
But when society close the door
I found myself dreaming no more

Tell me what does this mean
I try very hard from the start
I pay my dues
Always refused
What can I say?
I always pray
It's up to me to choose

I want to live
My time I give
I'm tired of being used
I am a man
Love me if you can
My intentions are good
Misunderstood
That's why I keep the blues

Oh! By the way
I can see today
God showed me the way

Gone Fishing

My brother Leroy loved to fish
Fishing season we did not miss
Up every morning before sunrise
Standing in water above our thighs

Waiting for the fish to bite
Fishing lines, stretched very tight
We love Mother Nature in every way
She loved us back everyday

We would catch fish all day long
It would get dark before going home

When daddy saw the whole lot
He'd go to the kitchen
To get the grease hot

We would all clean fish
Then daddy would pray
He'd thank the Lord for a blessed day

Happiness

The hard times are over
The storm has gone away
The sun is shinning brightly
It is such a lovely day

The winds of time are changing
The sky is very clear
The children are busy playing
They're happy to be here

Forget about your worries
Forget about the bad
Cast away your anger
And the things that make you sad

Set you mind on goodness
Forget about the past
Live you r life in peace
Happiness can last

Heart Broken

I came back to life this morning
I forgot the hurt and pain
I didn't worry about my sorrows
I have found myself again

I drifted back from darkness
I conquered hurt and fear
I rose above adversity
I am happy to be here

The sun is shinning again
The storm has gone away
I can laugh loud my friend
It is such a beautiful day

Hell's Hollow

For those without faith
The world is the gate
A place where man controls
No regard for the soul
He carries the torch of hate
The hollow forever waits

He has no love for God
His way forever hard
He dug his own grave
Believers shall be saved

Deep in a dark dreary hole
The doomed lost soul
Things of the world will not be enough
On the edge of the hollow there's a great gulf
Trapped are the sinners
Forever they shall dwell
In the pit of HELL

Homeless

The landfill is full of trash today
Bygone matters thrown away
Sofas and chairs
A rusty pair of stairs
The food covers the ground

Back in the city the homeless walk around.
Looking for food in garbage cans
Dreams nowhere to be found
Left on the corner to bum a meal
Trade it for a drink—told a lie
That's no big deal

Cardboard box to lay my head:
Finish the bottle
Or share with Fred

Went to the welfare office today
Took a number to wait my turn
Many people in the way
Money you need to earn

Dropped by the Salvation Army to eat
Found some shoes for my feet
The water in the shower is hot today
Cut the grass to get some pay
Finish the job just before noon
Told the captain - see you soon.

Judgement

If you don't know the way
You cannot know the day
When the sun fails to shine
When the wind goes astray

When the mountains crumble down
When there's no whisper or sound

When the lights all go out
When times turns about
When the sky turns gray
When there's no more to say

When the angels take control
Pray for you soul
When all saints are in
The final day of sin

Life

Sometimes the way is easy,
Sometimes the way is hard.
God had the answer from the very start.
It seems very clear, it's him we should fear.
He was in the beginning,
He is here with us now.
He will be here tomorrow,
He cares about our sorrows.
He understands our weakness,
He recognizes our pain,
He gave us hope in Jesus,
Forever he shall reign

Lost and Found

Moving to the city to find my dream
Looking for fame and glory
This place is really crowded! Big it seems
They all know the story

Had some money yesterday
Don't know how it got away
Found a job in the store
They had no one to clean the floor

Trying my best to hold a job
Life up here is getting hard
Think about home everyday
Down their things don't be this way

Try to hold out best I can
People don't speak up here you know
Cut my hand with a sharp knife
Did not listen to mama's advice
Going down the hall to use the phone
Hello mama, can I come home?

Love

Love is a word that is very strong
It can separate right from wrong

It brings us together in a special way
It should be first in your mind everyday

It is no sacrifice
It can find you a mate
It overrides hate
It brings great joy
Sometimes it hurts

It can be like heaven when two people share
Everything seems right when love is there

It can be taught
It hides all faults
It excepts wrong
There is sorrow when it's gone

God so loved the world he gave his only son
Love will stand the test of time
After everything is done

Chapter VI

Midnight Dream

One day the great eagle come from far above.
His eyes were fire, his talons like gloves.
His wings covered the sky above

Upon a mountain he sat down.
The golden rings around his head looked like a crown.
He looked at the crowd of people, as they ran in fright.
But I moved forward to see this great sight.

He raised his wings and to my surprise,
There were two angels I could not believe my eyes
Down to the earth they began to fly.
The female angel was carrying the male.
He was battered and weak his skin was so pale.

She laid him down at my feet.
I tried to talk to him but he could not speak.
I called for help, they came right away.
I could not believe this is such a great day.
God has chosen me to lead the way.

Mother Edwards

One day I met a lady that had a beautiful smile,
She treated me so nice I decided to hang around a while.

She reminded me of a lady that I knew long ago,
That lady was my mother; I really miss her so.

I was told that when you age your step; get slow,
Someone needs to tell her, I don't think she know.

As the days and months go by, she never change her ways,
To me she will always be special all of my days.

If I have a problem no matter what it is,
After talking to her, it helps to ease my fears.

I don't remember a day that she treated me like a stranger,
I pray that God will always keep her
from hurt, harm, and danger.

When her time is over on this side of the river,
God has a home that he is going to give her.

Someday across the river, above the great beyond,
God will call her name Jimmie "Lee Frog" Edwards
Job Well Done!

No Respect for Person

You may be a king
You may be a queen
You may be a preacher
Or a very good teacher

You may have the knowledge of a universe
You may be tall
Or even small
Remember God is first

All knowledge and wisdom
All glory and fame
Free or in prison
Life is not a game

Stop the chatter
It's a serious matter
You have yourself to blame
Open your eyes
To your surprise
He made all of us the same

Peace

After the flesh, yield to the spirit
After the mind is set free
After your life has come full circle
You can stand tall like a tree

The wind cannot uproot you
The things of this world are made clear
The life that you have is very dear

All of our days are numbered
Our time is not long

When God wakes you from slumber.
Another great day is gone

We live our days one at a time
It is such a great joy to have peace of mind.

Revelation

When the sun refuses to shine
When the rain turn away,
When life as we know it, has its final day
When all the people living have no more to say
Then time everlasting will make its play

The people are sleeping
Believers are weeping
The hour is minutes away
There is time to repent
There is time to pray
Get on your knees
Say Father please let me join you today

He is alpha-omega
The only everlasting there's no surpassing
His love and his mercy
There are none equal to stand in his way.

Seasons Change

When the leaves turn brown its fall
The sky turns blue or gray
When the birds change their call
Winter is own its way

After the snow, ice and cold
Springs comes in so bold
The trees are tall and green
The flowers smell so sweet
God thank you for spring

The fruit will grow in the heat
The grass is growing everywhere
The lovers are holding hands
The bees are getting the share
The kids are playing in the sand

Summer days are hot
You find a cool spot.

Show me the Way

It woke up early this morning
I thanked God for the letting me live
I see the new day dawning
Time is not ours to give

I asked God to bless me today
To keep me in his hand
He can show you the way
Please don't follow man

Man has no control
He's unworthy, arrogant and bold
He's does not know the way
God wants your soul.

The Spirit of the Wind

The wind is a stranger to all mankind
It blows where it listeth for all time

It takes out the old
It brings in the new
It brings in the cold
It drives up the dew

It control the seasons
It brings in the storm,
You will never see it in any shape or form

You cannot catch it,
It is young and old
Likewise is the spirit of every man's soul.

Sunrise

From dark to light
The sky turns bright
The birth of a new day

The people got up late
Time has its way
Who knows what's the fate?
No one knows the way

Be happy your eyes are open
Thank God for your blessing
The word has been spoken
We all were transgressing

The new day will be testing
Get up and face the world
Every man, woman, boy, and girl.

The Battle for the Soul

The flesh was formed from dirt
The Spirit gave it birth
From the very start,
They both were worlds apart

One was condemned; the other set free
The flesh is the cause of all misery

The flesh is sinful, the spirit is divine
One shall ruled the other, in the course of time

Lust, greed, and selfishness cause the flesh to sin
Love, obedience, and patience cause the spirit to win

If you allow the spirit to rule, your soul will be saved.
If you let the flesh control, your home will be the grave.

Chapter VII

The Eagle

The top of the sky where the eagle fly
Searching the ground below
Looking for a way to go
Strong and mighty are his ways
Very seldom is he seen
A bird of prey, so they say
Sent by God to lead the way

Have you seen the eagle today?
He flew into Egypt
America too
He freed the Hebrews
The believers knew
He is flying today – Oh, by the way!
The slaves saw him so they say

He sat on a mountain
He looked around
When souls were lost
He flew down
Remember the song as we sing
God will deliver on eagle wings

The Great Beyond

One day we'll cross the river
To the land of no return
You want need gold or silver
Money will be no concern

This place will be your home
Forever we shall roam
No matter what we say
We cannot come back this way

Faith we cannot buy
Your home is waiting on high
Open to young and old
The Valley is calm and green
The streets are made of gold
There's a life giving stream
There's peace for your soul

The Great Lie

When your heart is full of trouble
When all you feel is pain
When everything is in both
Hurt will remain

Evil thoughts come to you
You hate your very name
You walk in dark shadows
You have no claim to fame

You live your life in darkness
Every day is the same
You have a lonely feeling
You have nowhere to go
You forget the God that made you
You knock on hell's door

The devil will entertain you
He'll make your life a mess
He will promise you the world
He will offer you the best
He will cause you to suffer
Your soul will never rest

The Only Way to Go

Born in a world full of hate and sin,
Life is a fight that you must win.
You should keep your eyes on God,
Also, trust in his son.

You must work all day until the work is done.
You should look towards heaven,
which comes your help.
You must love one another with every step.

You must keep the commandments everyday.
You have to be sincere, when you pray.
You should not worry about everyday's tolls and strife.
Keep your mind on Jesus let him be your life.

Jesus came to this world to set all of us free.
He lived a perfect life for everyone to see.

Now when your life is over on this side of the river.
God has a home that he is going to give you.
One day across the river above the great beyond,
God will call your name servant well done.

The Sparrow

A small little bird
Seldom heard
It has a place
In the time of space

It makes its nest
Among the rest
The eggs are small
The trees are tall

Sometimes they all cover the whole tree
They have no worry, in no hurry
God watches over them
He watches over me

The Truth

Sometimes we close our eyes
Sometimes we walk away
Sometimes we make excuses
Something are hard to say

We rather live a lie
Or find an alibi
We refuse to see the light
We struggle day and night

We cannot really see
The truth will set you free
We try hard to be excepted.
We hate to be alone
We want everyone to like us
Although your self-respect is gone

The world is full of trouble
The people cold as ice
Jesus is the answer
He made the sacrifice

He died for you to live
He set your soul free
They nailed him to a cross
For the whole world to see

The grave could not hold him
Time cannot erase
He came on a mission
He is God's holy grace.

The Valley

The grass is tall and green
Flowers all around
There is water in the stream
Flowing to the ground

The mountains looking down
The clouds are up above
Such beauty never found
The wonders of his love

In the mist there's a garden
Fruits of all kind
When the way hardens
There's peace there to find

This place we all may share
The master really cares.

Time is Running Out

If your life is unhappy
Full of worries and doubt
There is no need to bother
Time is running out

If you're in a hurry
If you're running away
If you need some shelter
There is no such place today

All that's done is done
The battle has been won
The victory is not the grave
Blessed are the saved

Pray for the lost
Sin was the cost
On that final day
Every soul shall pay
Don't worry about the years
God shall wipe away your tears.

Time

Before the earth was formed
Before the universe
The mystery of time was first
It was with God in the beginning
It's here with us now
There's no searching its origin
We don't know where or how

It visits everyday in a very special way
It gives freely when we sleep, work, or play
It's here when you are right
It's here when you are wrong
It changes not, so clever
It will be here when you are gone

Vanity

Money is not the answer
The world is not the way
You will leave these things behind you
There is a final day

No matter what you own
No matter what you buy
All of this is vanity
There are treasures in the sky

There is a place up there, full of silver and gold
A place everlasting
A home for your soul

Vengeance

When people do wrong
Don't seek revenge
Separate yourself
Fences do mend

Vengeance is mine says the Lord
I have fought your battles
From the start

Moses met Pharaoh at the sea one day
Joshua fought the Battle of Jericho-David wouldn't let anything
get in his way
Jesus taught all of us how to pray

Giddeen stood on the battlefield
On Easter Day the world stood still
Samson was a mighty man
Lazarus was raised from the grave
Through Jesus Christ - the world was saved

You may say this story is old.
Maybe you say it shouldn't be told.
God has power over heaven and earth.
This story was true before your birth.

Victory

They marched him to a hill.
He said it was not his will.
They nailed him to a tree
He set the captives free.

They hated him from the start
He loved them from the heart
They pierced him in the side
Crowned his head with thorns
All that love him cried.
Some of them even mourned.

He cried out loud and bold.
For God to take his soul
When the crowd gathered around,
He looked down to the ground.

He told his mother don't weep
From a voice so deep
You asked the reason why
Did he have to die
He died that we may live
With all his love to give

They laid him in a grave
Blessed are the saved.
In three days he rose
The grave could not hold.

The victory belongs to God.
Triumphant from the start
Now all can be saved.
From the sting of the grave
Oh! By the way
He rose on Easter Day.